YAMAHA BAND STUDENT

BAND METHOD FOR GROUP OR INDIVIDUAL INSTRUCTION

by

ohn O'Reilly
ohn Kinyon

Welcome to Book 3 of the YAMAHA BAND STUDENT.

our completion of Books 1 and 2 show that you have worked hard and ade wonderful progress toward becoming an accomplished musician.

he YAMAHA BAND STUDENT Book 3 will provide you with continued rowth in developing a foundation for your future in music: as a composer, ck musician, teacher, conductor, symphony musician or a listener enjoying e life-long benefits of music.

our teacher's special skills, a fine instrument, your personal commitment d the YAMAHA BAND STUDENT is all it takes.

John O'Reilly

John Kinyon

Instrumentation

Flute
Oboe
Bassoon
B♭ Clarinet
E♭ Alto Clarinet
B♭ Bass Clarinet
E♭ Alto Saxophone
B♭ Tenor Saxophone
E♭ Baritone Saxophone
B♭ Trumpet / Cornet
Horn In F
Horn in E♭
Trombone
Baritone T.C.
Baritone B.C.
Tuba
Percussion—S.D., B.D., Access.
Keyboard Percussion
Combined Percussion
Piano Accompaniment
Piano Accompaniment Cassette
Conductor's Score

YAMAHA®
is a registered trademark of
Yamaha Corporation of America

TRUMPET FINGERING CHART

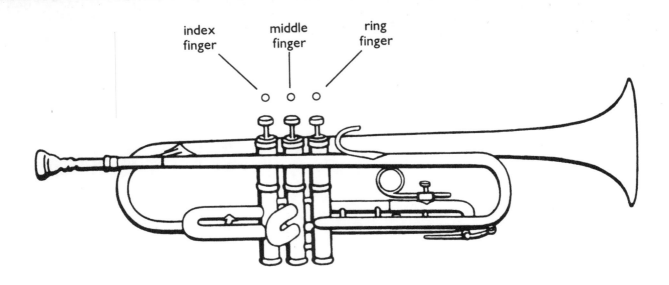

index finger   middle finger   ring finger

○ = valve up
● = valve down

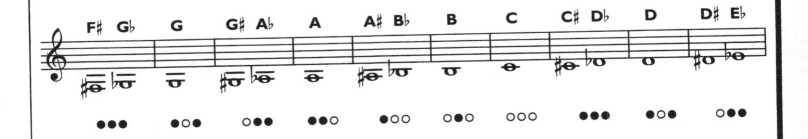

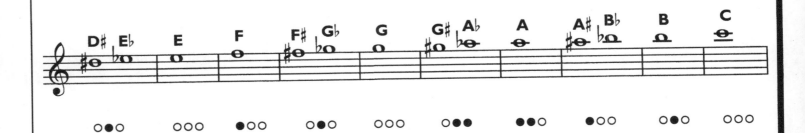

THE PARTS OF THE TRUMPET

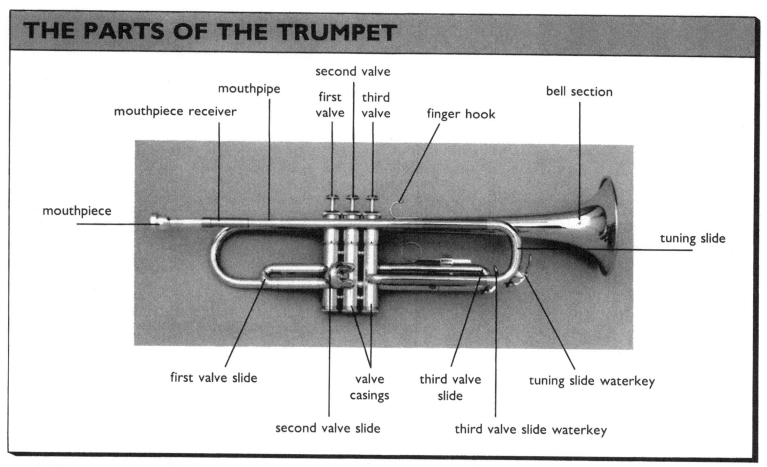

STUDENT'S PRACTICE CHART

Name _____ To become a good musician you must practice every day. Find a convenient place where you can keep your instrument, book, music stand and any other practice equipment. Try to practice at the same time every day.

Week	MON	TUES	WED	THURS	FRI	SAT	SUN	Approval	Week	MON	TUES	WED	THURS	FRI	SAT	SUN	Approval
1									19								
2									20								
3									21								
4									22								
5									23								
6									24								
7									25								
8									26								
9									27								
10									28								
11									29								
12									30								
13									31								
14									32								
15									33								
16									34								
17									35								
18									36								

Review of all keys and rhythms taught
in Yamaha Band Student Books 1 and 2.

C Major Etude and Chords
(B♭ Major Concert)

A Minor Etude and Chords
(G Minor Concert)

F Major Etude and Chords
(E♭ Major Concert)

D Minor Etude and Chords
(C Minor Concert)

G Major Etude and Chords
(F Major Concert)

E Minor Etude and Chords
(D Minor Concert)

B♭ Major Etude and Chords
(A♭ Major Concert)

G Minor Etude and Chords
(F Minor Concert)

D Major Etude and Chords
(C Major Concert)

6

Dixie

Pilgrims Chorus

WAGNER

Beautiful Dreamer

Duet

FOSTER

FULL BAND ARRANGEMENT

The Phantom March

9

10

$\frac{5}{4}$ = 5 beats to a measure

$\frac{5}{4}$ = quarter note gets 1 beat

Struttin'
Duet

Moderato

El Relicario

PADILLA

Vivace

B MINOR
(A minor Concert)

TEMPO

Andantino
Faster than Andante

1

Trumpet Tune

CLARKE

Andantino

f

mp

mf

f

rit.

God Rest Ye, Merry Gentlemen

3 Moderato

mf

Add the Bar Lines—Then Clap the Rhythm

4

Lonesome Cowboy
Duet

FULL BAND ARRANGEMENT

Barnacle Bill the Sailor

14

Theme from Symphony #5

TCHAIKOVSKY

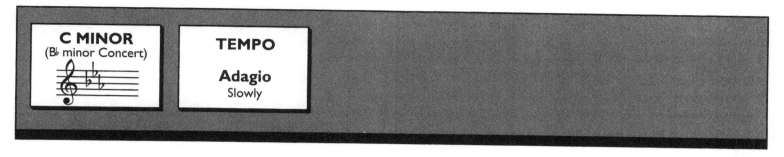

C Minor Scale and Chords
(B♭ Minor Concert)

Minor Portrait

Swingin' Along
Duet

March of the Three Kings

16

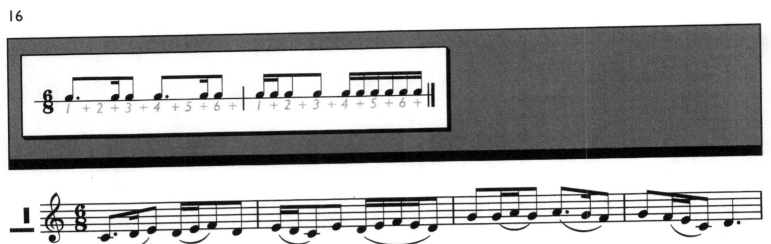

Believe Me If All Those Endearing Young Charms

Canonic Variations
Duet

TALLIS

FULL BAND ARRANGEMENT

A Christmas Lullaby

Procession of the Sardar

IPPOLITOV-IVANOV

Cake Walk

DEBUSSY

20

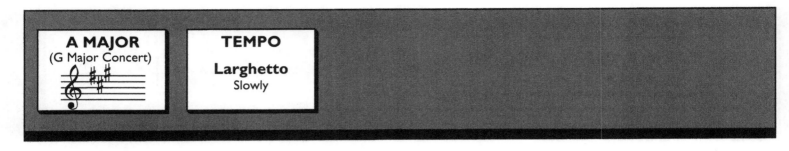

A Major Scale and Chords
(G Major Concert)

Greensleeves

Country Gardens

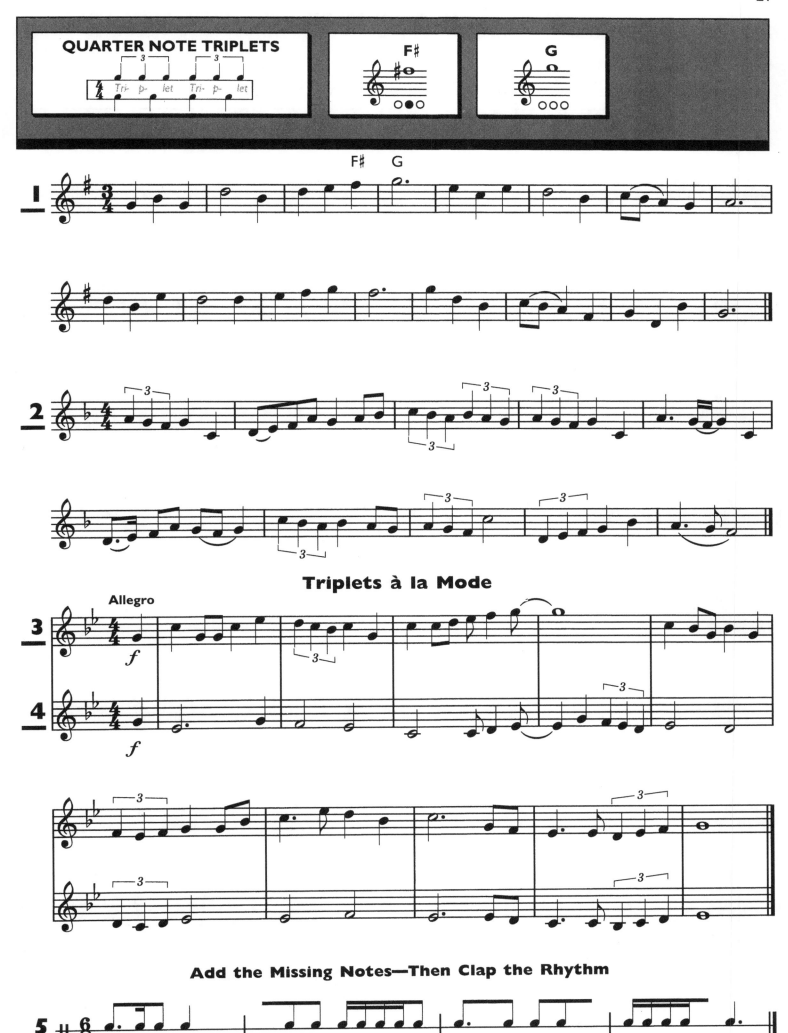

La Donna è Mobile

Duet

VERDI

FULL BAND ARRANGEMENT

Mardi Gras Strut

24

CHANGING TIME SIGNATURES

Funeral March of a Marionette

GOUNOD

Allegretto

Medieval Dance

Duet

Adapted from
JOHN ADSON

TRUMPET SOLO

The Bluebells of Scotland

FULL BAND ARRANGEMENT

Suite for Winds and Percussion

Finale

30

E Melodic Minor
(D Minor Concert)

A Melodic Minor
(G Minor Concert)

D Melodic Minor
(C Minor Concert)

B♭ Major
(A♭ Major Concert)

G Melodic Minor
(F Minor Concert)

YAMAHA BAND STUDENT

CERTIFICATE
OF ACHIEVEMENT

YAMAHA BAND STUDENT

has successfully completed Book Three
of the Yamaha Band Student.

_____
Band Director

_____
Date

_____
Authors